MEASUREMENT OF RESPONSIBILITY

Published in the U.S.A.
by Halsted Press, a Division
of John Wiley & Sons Inc.,
New York

Library of Congress Cataloging in Publication Data

Jaques, Elliott.
    Measurement of Responsibility.

"A Halsted Press book."
Includes bibliographical references.
    1. Wages.   2. Job evaluation.   3. Responsibility.
I. Title.
HD4915.J3   1972   331.2'2   72-5856
ISBN 0-470-44020-1

Printed in Great Britain by
Biddles Ltd, Guildford, Surrey, England

PREFACE

ALTHOUGH this book was first published fifteen years ago, it still gives the best account of how the time-span method of measuring responsibility in work was first developed. Both the description of the research and the theoretical considerations still stand. Any changes which have taken place are in the refinement in method of time-span measurement. These refinements are described in *Time-Span Handbook*.*

The description in the Introduction of how this book was published will explain why it is a difficult task to acknowledge the assistance I have received with its preparation. Many hundreds of individuals in the firm have been directly involved in the work that has led up to it. Each of the discussions we have had and the reports they have worked through have their repercussions in these pages. I should like to mention those who were members of the firm's Works Council during the course of the work described, as the means of acknowledging the contribution of the individual members they represented, as well as the work they contributed in their roles as representatives.

The members of the Works Council were:

Mr. W. B. D. Brown—Managing Director. *Grade I Staff Members:* Mr. P. G. Forrester, Mr. R. Joy, Mr. P. D. Liddiard. *Grade II Staff Members:* Mr. A. E. Burke, Mr. J. Horne, Mr. C. Le Blond, Mr. A. G. Oram, Mr. R. Salter,

---

* Elliott Jaques, *Time-Span Handbook*, Heinemann, London, 1964.

v

Mr. K. Seymour, Mr. F. Shaw, Mr. H. G. Wisher. *Grade III Staff Members:* Mr. W. H. Crittenden, Mr. M. J. Coviello, Mr. F. I. Flack, Mr. R. W. Knott, Mr. A. J. Kroneck, Mr. E. C. Lucking, Mr. D. E. Nichols, Mr. J. W. Valentine, Mr. A. M. Wardrop. *Works Committee Members:* Mr. A. E. Bond, Mr. A. G. Cannon, Mr. L. A. Carran, Mr. T. C. Challinger, Mr. F. Cooper, Mr. J. Dalziel, Miss R. Healey, Mr. S. J. Healy, Mr. G. C. Hefford, Mr. T. Hungerford, Mr. W. H. Morton, Mr. G. Nicholas, Mr. J. A. Radley, Mr. F. G. Woods.

The officers of the Works Council during this period were: Dr. G. H. Gange—Chairman; Miss R. Fowler and Mr. J. West—Secretaries.

Of the above members of the Works Council, the following were in addition members of the Steering Committee of the Council, which was responsible for the work of the social-analyst:

Dr. G. H. Gange—Chairman; Miss R. Fowler, Mr. J. West—Secretaries; Mr. P. G. Forrester, Mr. W. H. Morton—Vice-Chairmen; and Mr. T. C. Challinger, Mr. P. G. Forrester, Mr. E. C. Lucking, Mr. W. H. Morton, Mr. G. Nicholas, Mr. A. G. Oram, Mr. A. M. Wardrop, Mr. F. G. Woods.

In addition, I must refer to the special help I have had from certain members who have worked on the manuscript. Mr. D. J. Clarkson, Mr. E. C. Lucking, Mr. W. H. Morton, Mr. G. Nicholas, have read and carefully criticized parts of it, and I have incorporated many of their suggestions. To Mr. W. B. D. Brown and Mr. J. M. M. Hill I must add further thanks for the painstaking manner in which they have gone through the whole of the manuscript in draft form. Their comments have been the source of some major revisions as well as many minor ones.

Miss Rhoda Fowler, who typed the manuscript, has done much more than secretarial work. She has been involved in many of the events described in her capacity as secretary to the Works Council, and its Steering Committee. Her know-

MEASUREMENT OF RESPONSIBILITY

A Study of Work, Payment, and Individual Capacity

ELLIOTT JAQUES

A HALSTED PRESS BOOK

JOHN WILEY & SONS
New York

ledge and experience thus gained, and her genuine and cooperative interest, have been of the greatest help in preparatory work, and in assuring the accuracy of the description.

CONTENTS

INTRODUCTION

I

THE industrial scene continues to be disturbed by recurring difficulties in settling wage disputes in the absence of a defined wage and salary structure. The methods to be described herein might be considered to suggest a possible route towards a systematic pattern of financial reward in relation to the level of work done. These methods have been developed in the course of social consultancy work carried out in conjunction with a London engineering factory.

This consulting work has followed on from an applied social research project carried out in the same factory[1] between 1948 and 1951—financed by a Government research grant. The purpose of this research had been to explore in depth various aspects of industrial life within a single industrial unit. During this research phase, a number of changes had occurred in the Company, changes to which the research had contributed in such work as: an analysis and work-through of the problem of changing from piece-rates to flat rates in one department; an analysis of the work

---

[1] The Company is the Glacier Metal Company, and the work in the research phase—carried out in collaboration between the Company and a research team from the Tavistock Institute of Human Relations—has been reported in Elliott Jaques, *The Changing Culture of a Factory* (London: Tavistock Publications, 1951), and in articles in the journal *Human Relations*, contributed by A. K. Rice, J. M. M. Hill, E. L. Trist, and Elliott Jaques.

and functions and responsibilities of the Company's Works Council and representative organization; analyses, carried out at their request, on problems experienced by such diverse groups as the Works Committee, an executive group known as the Superintendents' Committee, and the top management group.

At the end of this period, when the Government research grant finance came to an end, the Company decided to carry on for itself the kind of work that had been done. It was the unanimous conclusion of its Works Council[1] that the work that had been done up till that time had been of practical benefit to the Company. They were in favour of continuing on a limited scale to see what further results might be achieved. The plan ultimately adopted was that the author should act on a part-time basis as a consulting social-analyst, responsible to the Works Council. This relationship, which is considered in detail in the next section, continues at the present time.

With the start of the new relationship in January 1952, there was a continuation of work on the above lines. Among the projects undertaken were, for example, an extensive analysis of the Company's total executive organization; the continuation of work with representative bodies; and work with a planning group charged with the responsibility to design and develop a management-training programme. There had been a striking absence of contact, however, with a range of problems—openly recognized in the firm—having

---

[1] The Company's Works Council is a body comprising fourteen members: the Managing Director plus thirteen elected members representative of the hourly-rated operators and the various grades of staff. Its Chairman is an independently elected member. The Company's policy requires that the Works Council shall consider any matters whatever. Agreement on the Council must be by unanimous decision, and no changes in the policy considered by the Council are made without this unanimous agreement. In the absence of such agreement, the previous policies or established precedents are continued. Cf. Chapter V, *The Changing Culture of a Factory* for a description of the development of the Council's policy-making responsibility and its mode of operation.

to do with status and grading, and with staff salaries and hourly-rated wages. Then, in September 1952, the work done with the Company radically changed in this respect. This change came about as a result of a request from an elected committee representing a section of the staff, to help it with an analysis of its own views about staff status and grading. The project, which thus started as a limited analysis of salary structure, status, and grading as it affected one section of the staff, eventually grew into an analysis of salary and wage differentials, status and grading, and promotion, selection, and appointments procedures, as these affected the Company as a whole. In order to appreciate how this development occurred, and to assess the findings from it, it will be necessary to understand the particular nature of the working relationship between the social-analyst and the members of the Company.

II

The relationship between the consultant and the firm was defined, after many months of discussion, in a document finally adopted by the Works Council in October 1952. This document laid down that he should be responsible to the Works Council through its Steering Committee—the Steering Committee being the executive committee of the Council, acting on its behalf between meetings. His responsibilities were defined as providing such professional services as might assist the working of the Company's organization. These professional services included: research on behalf of the Steering Committee; technical assistance on problems of social organization and group relations to members in their executive roles or as representatives, or to executive or representative groups or committees; assistance in a work-through role to groups who wished either to examine their own relationships in a general way, or to tackle difficulties in relationships that might be standing in the way of efficient work or progress.

A matter of considerable interest and importance was to discover means whereby the professional independence of the social-analyst could be assured. His contract was established on an annual basis, running from January to December. It was to be reviewed in June each year, so that if it was decided to terminate the contract there would be a six-month period during which any active work could be completed. Because wage and salary levels were not matters of public discussion in the firm (a matter that eventually became of some importance in the work to be reported), a special mechanism was devised for settling fees. The fee paid was to be set by the Managing Director, within terms of reference agreed in the Council as to the comparable executive level at which payment should be fixed. The point of this contract was to define the social-analyst's position not as a member of the Company but as somebody outside the Company who was available to assist any of its members. The contract has been reviewed and continued on this basis each year since that time. The review is by the Company's Works Council, it being a condition of the contract that the members of this body should be unanimously in accord for the contract to continue for another year.

The independence of role has been further defined by the conditions established for the social-analyst's work within the factory. Any section of the Company, or any member, or group of members, may apply directly to him for his services. Work can proceed so long as it has the endorsement of those immediately concerned, either directly or through their representatives acting on their behalf. Complete confidentiality is maintained. The members of the group concerned can talk about whatever they wish; the social-analyst for his part confining himself to analysing what is said—commenting on relationships within the immediate group, and on their discussion, to aid understanding and working-through of the difficulties—but most definitely not discussing any